The Life Story of Louis Zamperini

The Unbroken Biography of an Athlete and a World War Survivor

Luminarity Press

All rights reserved. Without the publisher's prior written consent, no portion of this publication may be copied, distributed, or transmitted in any way, including by photocopying, recording, or other mechanical or electronic means, with the exception of brief quotations used in critical reviews and other noncommercial uses allowed by copyright law.

The information used in this book was compiled from several internet sources. A lot of effort has gone into making sure that the information contained in this work is accurate and trustworthy. Nevertheless, the publisher and author cannot ensure that the information provided here is entirely accurate or comprehensive due to the dynamic nature of internet material.

Copyright © 2024 Luminarity Press

Table of Contents

Table of Contents	2
Introduction	4
Chapter 1	10
Early Years	10
Chapter 2	13
The 1936 Olympics Participation	13
Louis's Post-Olympic Career	15
Survival and Capture	18
Zamperini's Evangelism	20
Chapter 3	23
Awards and Legacy	23
Academic Recognition	24
Broader Impact	25
Net Worth	26
Charity Work	26
Chapter 4	29
Personal Life	29
Sibling Support	29
Bully's Prey	30
A Brush with Death	30
Delinquent to Devoted Athlete	31
Finding Love & Building a Family	31
Death	33
Chapter 5	34

Louis Zamperini Untold Tales   **34**
   The "Unbroken" Controversy   34
   Zamperini's Odyssey   35
   Japan's WWII Legacy   37
   Global Reaction to History   39
   Zamperini's Troubled Youth   40
   Zamperini's Olympic Exploit   41
   Zamperini's Survival Ordeal   44
   Zamperini's Saving Journey   47
   Zamperini's Forgiveness Legacy   49
Conclusion   **51**

Introduction

Louis Silvie Zamperini, born on January 26, 1917, in Olean, New York, was the son of Italian immigrants. His journey into the world of athletics began during his time at Torrance High School in Torrance, California, where his talent for long-distance running became evident. In 1934, Zamperini set a remarkable national high school mile record of four minutes and twenty-one seconds, a record that stood unbroken for two decades. His exceptional performance caught the attention of the University of Southern California, which awarded him a track scholarship.

Zamperini's Olympic aspirations were put on hold by World War II, but he had already tasted Olympic competition. He participated in the 1936 Berlin Games, where he competed in the 5,000 meters. Despite only training for a few weeks for the event, Zamperini impressed by finishing strong, with a final lap time of 56 seconds. At just 19 years old, he tied for first place with Don Lash, the current world record holder, in the 5,000-meter Olympic trials in

New York City, securing his spot at the Berlin Olympics.

With the outbreak of World War II, Zamperini's life took a dramatic turn. He served as a bombardier in the Army Air Corps and was involved in a crash that left him stranded at sea for 47 days. Eventually captured by the Japanese, Zamperini endured two years of brutal treatment as a prisoner of war, facing torture and deprivation.

After the war, Zamperini returned to the United States as a national hero. His remarkable story of survival, resilience, and redemption was documented in the 2014 book "Unbroken: A Story of Survival, Redemption, and Resilience in World War II." Zamperini's legacy extends beyond his athletic achievements, serving as an inspiration to many for his indomitable spirit and unwavering courage in the face of adversity.

Continuing his athletic career at the university level, Zamperini achieved another milestone in 1938 by setting a new record for the mile, clocking in at an impressive 4 minutes and 8.3

seconds. This record would stand for the next fifteen years, a testament to his remarkable skill and endurance on the track. Despite his achievements, Zamperini's plans to compete in the 1940 Olympics were thwarted by the outbreak of World War II.

Joining the Army Air Corps, Zamperini's life took a different turn as he became involved in military operations during the war. In May 1943, while on a mission to locate a downed pilot, his aircraft, a B-24 Liberator, experienced mechanical failure and crashed into the Pacific Ocean. Out of the eleven crew members, only Zamperini and two others survived the crash.

Stranded on a life raft in the middle of the Pacific Ocean, Zamperini and his companions faced a harrowing struggle for survival. For 47 days, they battled extreme heat, strafing runs by Japanese aircraft, circling sharks, and severe dehydration. Their only sources of sustenance were rainwater and birds that landed on their raft, which they caught and killed.

After drifting for over a month at sea, Zamperini and one of the surviving crew members, Russell Allen "Phil" Phillips, washed ashore on a remote island in Japanese-occupied territory. Despite their rescue from the sea, their ordeal was far from over as they were captured by Japanese forces and taken as prisoners of war.

Separated from Phillips, Zamperini endured unimaginable hardships in a series of prisoner-of-war camps. He faced constant physical and psychological abuse, including brutal beatings and starvation. Particularly cruel was a camp sergeant known as "the Bird," who singled out Zamperini for continuous maltreatment and violent outbursts.

Despite his suffering, Zamperini's status as a former Olympic athlete may have spared him from death, as the Japanese saw him as a potential propaganda tool.

During his nearly two years of captivity, the United States military officially declared Zamperini dead. However, his true fate was not revealed until the end of the war in 1945 when he finally regained his freedom and returned to America.

Upon his return, Zamperini faced profound challenges, struggling with the trauma of his experiences and turning to alcohol. His marriage to Cynthia suffered, and they were on the brink of divorce. Despite this, they remained married until her death in 2001. In 1949, Zamperini experienced a turning point when he attended a sermon by Billy Graham in Los Angeles, which inspired him to seek recovery and redemption.

One of the most remarkable aspects of Zamperini's story was his ability to forgive his captors. He went on to establish the Victory Boys Camp, providing a refuge for troubled youth. In 1950, during a visit to a Tokyo prison, Zamperini personally pardoned several of his former captors who were imprisoned for war crimes.

Zamperini's life story inspired two books, "Devil at My Heels" (1956 and 2003), and the bestselling "Unbroken: A Story of Survival, Resilience, and Redemption in World War II" by Laura Hillenbrand. In 2014, a film adaptation of "Unbroken," directed and produced by Angelina Jolie, brought

Zamperini's story to a wider audience. Jolie also produced the sequel, "Unbroken: Path to Redemption," released in 2018.

Louis Zamperini passed away on July 2, 2014, at the age of 97, due to pneumonia. His legacy as a survivor, a hero, and a beacon of forgiveness and redemption continues to inspire people around the world.

Chapter 1

Early Years

Louis Zamperini, born on January 26, 1917, was the son of Anthony Zamperini, a native of Verona in northern Italy, and Louise Dossi, who hailed from Olean, New York. His family included two younger sisters, Sylvia and Virginia, and an elder brother named Pete. Raised in a strict and deeply religious Catholic household, Louis experienced a childhood marked by the values and traditions of his upbringing.

Despite the strong familial influence, Louis Zamperini's youth was not without its challenges. He began drinking and smoking at a young age, deviating from the expectations set by his family's beliefs. Additionally, he faced adversity in the form of bullies, surviving two near-death experiences. The first occurred during a house fire, and the second when he fell into an oil rig and nearly drowned. Throughout these trials, Pete, his older brother, remained a steadfast supporter, encouraging Louis in his athletic endeavors.

When little Louis Zamperini was two years old, his family relocated and settled in Long Beach, California, from Olean, New York. After relocating to neighbouring Torrance in 1919, Louis enrolled at Torrance High School.

Bullies picked on him because of his Italian heritage and the fact that he and his family couldn't speak English when they relocated to California. For self-defense purposes, his father instructed him in boxing.

He was soon boasting that he was "beating the tar out of every one of them," but he actually began to enjoy the prospect of exacting revenge. He felt like he needed it constantly.

While his older brother Pete was already a success on the school track team, he enrolled Zamperini to keep him out of trouble as a rebel. Zamperini had previously been challenged to a footrace by his classmates in ninth grade.

Coming in last, Louis was embarrassed. Pete went on multiple runs with Louis as a trainer. As his speed increased, Zamperini started winning races. Running long distances became Louis's passion after he met his hero, Glenn Cunningham.

During his first year of high school, he ran the 660-meter dash, which was the 600-meter event, and placed fifth in the city. From his first cross-country race that summer of 1932 through his final three years of high school, he ran without a loss.

His brother's records began to fall to him. At the 1934 California state championships preliminary meeting, he ran the mile in 4 minutes, 21.2 seconds, setting a new interscholastic record. His time of 4 minutes and 27.8 seconds won the CIF California State Meet championships the following week.

He was able to secure a full scholarship to USC because to that record. While attending the University of Southern California, he was a member of the Kappa Sigma fraternity's Delta Eta chapter.

Chapter 2

The 1936 Olympics Participation

Zamperini made the decision to participate in the 1936 Olympics. Athletes back then had to shell out their own cash to attend the Olympic trials, but Louis was able to secure a free train ticket thanks to his father's job with the railway. Merchants from Torrance pooled their resources to ensure the local hero could stay put once he arrived.

That year, Glenn Cunningham—who would go on to win the silver medal—as well as Archie San Romani and Gene Venzke all battled for a berth on the 1,500-meter relay squad. Instead of competing in the 1,500 metres, Zamperini ran the 5,000 metres.

Norm Bright, a fan favorite, and a number of others passed out on one of the warmest days of the year in 1936 at Randall's Island, New York, as part of the North American heat wave. Just in Manhattan that week, 40 individuals reportedly perished due to the heat.

Zamperini qualified for the 1936 Summer Olympics in Berlin, Germany, after finishing in a dead-heat tie with American record-holder Don Lash in the final sprint. At the age of 19 years and 178 days, he is still the youngest American to qualify for the 5,000-meter race.

It was widely assumed that neither Zamperini nor Lash had a chance of beating world record holder Lauri Lehtinen in the 5,000-meter run at the 1936 Olympics.

"He was a Depression-era kid who had never even been to a drugstore for a sandwich in his life," Zamperini recalled, "and all the food was free." He went on to narrate other stories from his Olympic experience, including his bingeing on the ferry ride to Europe.

His eyes were as big as saucers after eating seven sweet rolls with bacon and eggs every morning. Like the majority of the ship's athletes, Louis Zamperini had put on a significant amount of weight by the trip's end—specifically, 12 pounds (5 kilogrammes).

Even though putting on weight wasn't great for his running, he needed to do it for his health—he'd dropped 15 pounds (7 kilograms) practicing in New York City's summer heat for the Olympic Trials.

At the Olympics, Zamperini finished in eighth place in the 5,000-meter race, with a time of 14 minutes 46.8 seconds. The record-holder for the event, Lehtinen, was second, and Zamperini's colleague Lash, thirteenth.

The winner was Gunnar Höckert of Finland, who set the record with a time of fourteen minutes 22.2 seconds. Hitler shook Zamperini's hand and said, "Ah, you're the boy with the fast finish."

After Zamperini told him the story, Hitler had him come to his stand to continue the interview. His final lap of 56 seconds was fast enough to capture Hitler's attention.

Louis's Post-Olympic Career

Zamperini headed straight to USC after the Olympics to start his college career. His fraternity, Kappa Sigma (Delta-Eta Chapter), was active while he was a student at USC. Despite suffering serious injuries to his shins

15

from rivals who tried to spike him during the 1938 national collegiate mile (1609 meters) race, Zamperini set a record of 4 minutes 8.3 seconds; this record remained in effect for fifteen years, coining the nickname "Torrance Tornado."

After joining the US Army Air Force in September 1941, Zamperini was promoted to the rank of second lieutenant. On the Consolidated B-24 Liberator bomber Super Man, he was assigned the position of bombardier and sent to the island of Funafuti in the Pacific.

During a bombing mission in April 1943, Super Man and Zamperini attacked the island of Nauru, which was under Japanese control. Three Japanese Zeros attacked his bomber after the successful raid, badly damaging it.

One member of the crew passed away while five others were injured. On the return flight from the April 21 Nauru raid, Zamperini applied first aid to five wounded crew members of his Liberator bomber and saved the lives of two, according to the May 4 New York Times.

16

"Ground crewmen counted 500 bullet and shell fragment holes in the fuselage and tail structure of the big four-engine bomber after it had skidded to a stop with a flat tire."

Once Super Man was deemed unfit for flight, the crew members who were in good health were sent to Hawaii to be reassigned.

A hunt for a missing plane and its crew was assigned to Zamperini and a few other ex-Super Man crewmates. The Green Hornet, another B-24, was infamous among the pilots for being a flawed "lemon."

(According to aircraft records, there are multiple B-24s called "Green Hornet" or "The Green Hornet"; in this instance, the name was confirmed in Zamperini's pre-mission diary.) Louis sprinted a mile in under 4 minutes and 12 seconds in May 1943, just before his last mission.

Considering he was racing across sand, this is an incredible feat. Tragically, eight out of eleven soldiers on board perished in the bomber's fall into the seas 850 miles (1,370 km) south of Oahu on May 27, 1943, while the plane was searching.

Survival and Capture

With scarce supplies, the three survivors—Zamperini, pilot Russell Allen Phillips, and Francis McNamara—made do with rainwater, raw tiny fish, and birds that settled on their raft for sustenance.

Despite his first panic reaction and subsequent overindulgence in chocolate, McNamara made amends by rescuing the survivors from a shark attack while using an oar. Attempts to attract a search plane's notice were unsuccessful.

Two tiny rafts were released, and the guys managed to use the few tools they had recovered from the disaster. While fighting off relentless shark attacks and avoiding capsize due to a storm, they managed to catch two albatrosses—one of which they consumed—and utilised the other as bait to catch fish.

A Japanese bomber repeatedly strafed them, puncturing their life raft; yet, none of them were injured. When McNamara passed away after 33 days at sea, Phillips and Zamperini prepared to throw his body overboard.

After 47 days at sea, Zamperini and Phillips finally made it to the Marshall Islands, but the Japanese Navy promptly captured them. From the time they were captured in August 1945 until the war ended, they were subjected to brutal beatings and other forms of mistreatment. They were sent from Kwajalein Atoll to the Japanese prisoner-of-war camp at Ōfuna after 42 days, which was for captives who were not officially listed as POWs.

Zamperini was moved to the Ōmori POW camp in Tokyo after spending just over a year in Ofuna. He was later relocated to the Naoetsu POW camp in northern Japan, where he stayed until the war ended. Mutsuhiro "The Bird" Watanabe, a jail guard who tortured him, was later named one of the forty most sought Japanese war criminals by General Douglas MacArthur.

Boyington writes about the Italian recipes that Zamperini composed to distract the inmates from the food and conditions in his book Baa Baa Black Sheep. Zamperini and then-Major

Greg "Pappy" Boyington were both incarcerated at the same camp.

In terms of his postwar life, Zamperini was first reported missing at sea and then died in action one year and two days later.

A hero's welcome awaited him upon his return home. They had two children, Cissy and Luke, from their marriage to Zamperini in 1946 until Cynthia Applewhite passed away in 2001.

Zamperini's Evangelism

Cindy, his wife, became a born-again Christian after attending an evangelistic crusade in Los Angeles conducted by Billy Graham. Zamperini was persuaded to go on a crusade in 1949 by his Christian wife and friends.

He was hesitant, but eventually consented. Graham's sermon moved Zamperini to pledge his life to Christ, as it brought back memories of his prayers both on the life raft and in prison. After this, he was able to forgive his captors, and the dreams eventually stopped.

Graham later assisted Zamperini in beginning a new profession as a Christian evangelist. He visited numerous guards from his time as a prisoner of war to inform them that he had forgiven them; this was one of the themes that ran throughout his story.

Among these was a visit to Tokyo's Sugamo Prison in October 1950, where he met with incarcerated war criminals and offered them his pardon. Some others became Christians as a result, according to what Zamperini told CBN.

Zamperini ran a leg in the Olympic Torch relay for the Winter Olympics in Nagano, Japan, just four days before his 81st birthday in January 1998. Nagano was not far from the POW camp where he had been confined.

On that trip, he tried to meet with Mutsuhiro Watanabe, better known as "the Bird"—his chief and the most vicious enemy he had throughout the war—but Watanabe refused to meet with him. Despite this, Zamperini wrote to him to say that he had forgiven him despite the terrible treatment he had received from him.

Watanabe passed away in 2003, so it's unclear if he ever read the letter; Zamperini never heard back from him. Zamperini made his first trip back to Germany in March 2005 to see the Berlin Olympic Stadium, where he had participated, since his last visit.

Zamperini kept going to USC football games far into his 90s, and in 2009 he became friends with quarterback Matt Barkley. Zamperini discussed his life, the 1936 Olympics, and his WWII achievements during an appearance on Jay Leno's The Tonight Show with June 7, 2012.

Chapter 3

Awards and Legacy

There was more to Louis Zamperini's life than just athletics and the struggles of war. His impact is still felt many years after his death. The influence of these accolades, which recognize various aspects of the extraordinary man he became, is deeply ingrained in them.

The illustrious Louis Zamperini Invitational Mile, which takes place in the world-renowned Madison Square Garden, is a testament to his athletic prowess. This yearly competition is a tribute to his track skill and a way to immortalize his name.

In addition, being inducted into the National Italian American Sports Hall of Fame justly solidifies his legacy as a remarkable athlete who gave honor to his heritage.

The renaming of the airport to Zamperini Field is a towering symbol of civic pride in his birthplace of Torrance, California. Along with its passengers, every airplane carries a fragment of his life's narrative.

Just like that, Torrance High School's Zamperini Stadium is always there to show the next generation that greatness can come from anyone. He is now officially a hometown hero, and these accolades from his community will serve as an inspiration to generations of sportsmen to come.

Within Zamperini, the Olympic flame burned with unquenchable passion. Not only was he recognized for his athletic abilities, but his unfaltering attitude was powerfully symbolized by carrying the torch for the 1984 and 1998 Games. He exemplified the Olympic concept of tenacity and became a living embodiment of it.

Academic Recognition

The capacity to triumph over hardship had an impact well beyond the world of sports. Azusa Pacific University and Bryant University both presented him with honorary degrees to further recognize the profound insights he gained from his remarkable trip. These establishments saw the value in his story because it contained teachings about the power of the human spirit that went beyond mere physical achievements.

Broader Impact

The sphere of athletics was not the only one that Zamperini impacted. As the ceremonial first-pitch thrower at Major League Baseball games, his leadership and inspirational skills are on full display. His unassuming deed became an inspiration to those outside of the athletic world, who saw in him a symbol of perseverance and optimism. The Kappa Sigma Golden Heart Award is another recognition of his influence within the fraternal organization that is well-known for its commitment to brotherhood and service.

A deeper dive into Louis Zamperini's legacy will reveal more threads. We will explore further into the other accolades he received, including those that acknowledge his courage in WWII and the lasting influence his narrative has on people around the globe.

Net Worth

An American who survived captivity, ran the distance at the Olympics, and became an inspirational speaker, Louis Zamperini was worth $1 million. In January 1917, Louis Zamperini came into this world in Olean, New York. He left this world in July 2014. Unbroken: A World War II Story of Survival, Resilience, and Redemption, produced by Laura Hillenbrand in 2010, is a best-selling book that draws from Zamperini's experiences.

Charity Work

An understated thread of commitment to serving others merits acknowledgment, beyond the accolades and successes that characterized Louis Zamperini's life. The specifics of his post-war charitable endeavors are sketchy, but his life story indicates a man devoted to helping the downtrodden, especially at-risk youngsters.

He turned into a motivational speaker because of this commitment. Zamperini, who overcame his own issues, didn't do it for the sake of promoting his own story of forgiveness and strength. He used it to great effect, motivating and inspiring others in the audience, particularly the youth who were fighting their own struggles. He probably inspired other people to face adversity head-on and discover their inner strength by sharing his horrific experiences.

On top of that, it appears like at-risk children were Zamperini's primary target. This solidarity with causes that help the downtrodden is indicative of a profound understanding of the plight of the oppressed. Even though we may never know for sure which organizations he collaborated with, we can probably assume that he donated his time or took part in fundraisers for worthy causes.

His ability to motivate others to make a difference is further demonstrated by the story's lasting impression. Both the novel and the film adaptation of Unbroken were huge hits around the world, and their impact is still felt today. This never-ending source of motivation probably inspires people to do more than just get through tough times; it may even inspire

27

them to start their own philanthropic organizations.

Although additional research into interviews and historical documents may be necessary to fully understand Louis Zamperini's direct charitable work, what little is known about him suggests a man who, after overcoming immense personal tragedy, committed himself to helping others and providing hope to the downtrodden.

Chapter 4

Personal Life

From a difficult adolescence to an Olympic champion, Louis Zamperini's journey was everything but linear. Despite having a rocky relationship with his parents, his childhood was molded into the tenacious athlete and tenacious survivor he would become by a complicated family dynamic and his own defiant nature. Pete, his older brother, and two younger sisters made up his family. Although information is limited, it appears that Pete was instrumental in helping Louis realize his athletic potential by getting him to try out for the school's track team. The success that Louis would go on to achieve was probably laid by this caring friendship.

Sibling Support

Pete, his older brother, provided a ray of hope in the shape of sibling support. After seeing Louis's athletic prowess, Pete became his number one cheerleader and coach. An important decision that would shape Louis's career was his encouragement to focus on running, which he did. Through his unfaltering encouragement, Pete gave Louis direction in life, a means of expressing his emotions, and a chance to succeed.

Bully's Prey

Louis's defiance of parental and other authority figures wasn't his only point of rebellion. Additionally, he was the object of bullying. His competitive nature and need for self-promotion were probably stoked during this time. Perhaps the grit he honed learning to protect himself, maybe through his father's boxing classes, would have helped him weather the storms of war.

A Brush with Death

Stories from Louis's childhood describe a near-death experience he had in a house fire.

This terrifying event, along with another near-miss following a tumble into an oil rig, implies a degree of irresponsibility throughout his youth. These near-death experiences may have acted as an unconscious caution, leading him to pursue the seemingly safer route of competitive running.

Delinquent to Devoted Athlete

Under Pete's tutelage, Louis went from being a delinquent to a self-devoted athlete. His inherent ability on the track started to reveal itself. He had an incontestable amount of drive and desire on top of being lightning fast. This metamorphosis, spurred on by Pete's steadfast encouragement and Louis's personal need to prove himself, set the stage for the outstanding athletic accomplishments that were to follow.

Finding Love & Building a Family

Louis Zamperini discovered comfort and resilience in a love story that would last for more than fifty years, amidst the whirlwind of athletic victories and horrors of war. Louis wed Cynthia Applewhite in 1946, a young lady who would become his rock and the foundation of his family's life, only a year after he was freed from a Japanese prison camp. Even more importantly, the fact that they tied the knot in 1946 implies that they became close while Louis was extremely vulnerable. Upon his return from the war, he struggled to overcome the psychological and physiological effects of his captivity.

Nevertheless, their bond went beyond that of friends. As he faced the difficulties of his recovery, Cynthia was an anchor, a confidante, and a companion. Louis probably found the stability he sought in Cynthia's unfaltering love and patience as he fought his issues. Their joyous, loving existence together was a complete antidote to the tragedies he had faced.

The happy couple expanded their family with the arrival of a son, Luke, and a daughter, Cissy. They seem to share a want for stability and a future brimming with happiness and love in their decision to start a family. Even though Louis had a rocky connection with his parents growing up, he probably found great solace in providing for his own children and creating a strong family.

Death

The US government had incorrectly declared Zamperini dead while he was serving in World War II, classifying him as killed in action. A formal condolence card was even sent to Zamperini's parents by President Franklin D. Roosevelt in 1944. Zamperini was not found alive and released from his captors until the end of World War II in late 1945.

Seventy years later, on July 2, 2014, at the age of 97, Zamperini passed away at his home in Los Angeles from pneumonia.

Chapter 5

Louis Zamperini Untold Tales

The "Unbroken" Controversy

Naoetsu is a quiet coastal town where the American prisoner of war Louis Zamperini is placed in the war film Unbroken, directed by Angelina Jolie. He barely makes it through the ordeal of being bruised and starved by a cruel camp guard.

In 2010, Zamperini's narrative was transformed into a best-selling book and translated into thirty languages. Its themes revolve around courage and perseverance. Unbroken has been screened globally since its 2014 debut. Unless you count Japan, that is.

A right-wing campaign labelled the film as "anti-Japanese," which effectively halted its production. Some have criticised the film, claiming that it portrays Japanese soldiers in a racist light and that Angelina Jolie "hates" Japan.

A tiny indie distributor finally stepped in after more than a year of dispute, and the film will now have its premiere showing at an art house in the heart of Tokyo.

Extremists on the right have threatened to block the film's release in Japan by picketing the theater with sound trucks, which are vehicles outfitted with extremely loud speakers that can drown out all other sounds.

Zamperini's Odyssey

Zamperini, played by Jack O'Connell, was a long-distance runner who crossed paths with Adolf Hitler during his 1936 Berlin Olympics qualification. He managed to stay alive for 47 days on a raft in the Pacific before being caught by Japanese soldiers.

The majority of the leading critical and non-critical study on the war has come out of Japan, and the country's film studios have made several anti-war masterpieces. Foreign films depicting the abuse of prisoners of war, including those produced in the UK The country has screened Colin Firth and Nicole Kidman's The Railway Man.

Reflection, however, has long fought against official forgetfulness. No one in the Naoetsu area seemed to know anything about the camp or the fact that it was made famous in a Hollywood film. Nobody at the local library has ever heard of Zamperini.

"I don't think people care about something that happened so long ago," remarks Yukiko Ishida, a coffee shop owner situated half a mile from the site of the former camp. Though some claim to have known about the American prisoners in Japanese jails, others dispute this.

The lack of any kind of sympathetic Japanese character is the Achilles' heel of Unbroken. The film's portrayal of an Olympian's torture is unsettling, especially in a nation that is trying to avoid facing its history as it prepares to host the 2020 Summer Olympics.

Japan's WWII Legacy

According to Kinue Tokudome, the executive director of the US-Japan Dialogue on POWs, Zamperini was one of thirty thousand Japanese prisoners of war, and ten percent of that number perished.

"People don't know that history," she says with a grievance. In the countryside, they must have seen these malnourished white people. How did it slip their minds and prevent them from discussing it?

The Naoetsu camp was the site of around sixty Australian deaths between 1942 and 1945 as a result of illness and abuse. At the end of the war, more guards were tried and executed from this POW camp in Japan than from any other.

Mutsuhiro Watanabe, also known as "the Bird," the man who tortured Zamperini, was never punished, nevertheless. Where the camp formerly stood is now marked by a small park.

The memorial was erected in 1995 by members of the community in collaboration with relatives of incarcerated Australians. Unfortunately, many of the pioneers who battled for its construction have since died.

According to Mindy Kotler, director of the Washington-based think-tank Asia Policy Point, Japan's historical forgetfulness is intensifying under Prime Minister Shinzo Abe. There has been a complete and utter lack of accountability from the Abe administration about the conflict, she claims.

Japanese school textbooks were required earlier this year to reflect the government's stance on history and territorial problems, including a watering down of allusions to the war, per an order from the ministry of education.

By pledging to put a stop to Japan's humiliating apology diplomacy from the years following World War II, Mr. Abe has partially met a crucial demand of his followers. Japan "must not let... generations to come... be predestined to apologize," Mr. Abe said, refraining from expressing personal regret.

The decisions of the International Military Tribunal for the Far East (1946–1948) are currently being reviewed by an expert panel. Inada Tomomi, a close associate of Mr. Abe, stated that the convictions that led to the execution of Japan's six wartime commanders were "based on a poorly constructed" understanding of history.

Global Reaction to History

In reaction to Japan's revised textbooks, South Korea has announced that educators in the country will receive specialized training on the subject of Japan's military brothels during the war. History classes in China already cover the Japanese conquests of the 1930s and 1940s.

The lead character's embrace of reconciliation makes Unbroken a universally relatable story. Afterwards, Zamperini traveled to Japan to confront his kidnappers; he passed away in 2014 at the age of 97. He was chosen to carry the Olympic torch during the 1988 Nagano Olympics.

According to Ms. Tokudome, there is still a place in Japan to talk about the Great Depression and World War II, but she is concerned that this place is becoming smaller.

That young Japanese "have very few opportunities to learn about the history that took place in their country" is something she regrets.

Zamperini's Troubled Youth

Zamperini wasted his youth as a renowned troublemaker in Torrance, California, after being born to Italian immigrant parents in January 1917. His adolescent criminal enterprise was focused on stealing anything non-nailed down from neighbors and local businesses.

He started smoking at age 5 and started drinking at 8. Zamperini once threw tomatoes at a police officer, darkened the eyes of children who dared to question him, and caused a teacher's car tires to deflate after disciplining him.

He finally gave up on a life of minor crime while he was a high school track team member, much to the dismay of his family who thought he was destined for jail or homelessness.

He became one of the finest athletes in southern California after his older brother Pete encouraged him to do so. He set a national high school record for the mile run with a time of 4 minutes, 21 seconds.

Meeting with Adolf Hitler: Zamperini planned to compete in the 1936 Olympics after finishing high school. The "Torrance Tornado" became the youngest distance runner to ever make it to the Olympic team after making the switch from his favorite 1,500 meters to the 5,000 meters.

He had a strong performance at the U.S. trials. He finished seventh in his race at the Berlin Olympiad, which was held under the shadow of the growing Nazi power, when he was just nineteen years old. Despite his lack of experience, he won over the crowd with one of the fastest final circuits in the event's history.

Zamperini's Olympic Exploit

Adolf Hitler, who was among the amazed onlookers, leaned over from his box to shake Zamperini's hand and remarked, "Ah, you're the boy with the fast finish."

Despite receiving compliments from the German "Fuhrer," Zamperini nevertheless managed to get himself into a bit of a jam during the Olympics. He came dangerously close to being shot as he attempted to steal a Nazi flag from the Reich Chancellery as he left Berlin.

Zamperini became one of USC's most renowned student athletes after setting numerous records during his time there after an impressive performance at the 1936 Olympics.

Many started to whisper that Zamperini might be the one to break the 4-minute mile record, which was thought to be nearly impossible at the time. In 1938, Zamperini was named "the next mile champion" by former world record holder Glenn Cunningham; in 1939, he replied by running a perfect track season.

At the 1940 Olympics, he intended to compete for gold and possibly a miracle mile, but the competition was cancelled due to the onset of World War II. Zamperini joined the Army Air Corps in 1941 after having his Olympic aspirations momentarily thwarted.

Among Zamperini's WWII military duties was his time spent flying B-24 Liberator bombers with the 372nd Bomb Squadron of the Army Air Corps. Perched atop a jet dubbed "Super Man," he completed multiple missions from his perch.

One of these was the infamous December 1942 air raid on Wake Island, during which his plane returned to Midway Atoll on a limp due to a lack of fuel.

Several crewmen were severely wounded, and one was killed, when Japanese Zero fighter planes attacked Zamperini's B-24 during a subsequent bombing flight over the small island of Nauru.

The destroyed B-24 narrowly escaped catastrophe on an emergency landing at Funafuti island due to hydraulic fluid leaking. After the fact, Zamperini and his crewmates found out that their plane had over 600 holes in it due to shrapnel and enemy fire.

Zamperini's Survival Ordeal

During a search-and-rescue mission over the Pacific on May 27, 1943, Zamperini and his crew were airborne when their plane abruptly lost power to two engines and plummeted into the water. Zamperini, pilot Russell Allen Phillips, and tail gunner Francis McNamara were the only three survivors out of eleven crewmen.

The three of them spent weeks at sea in two life rafts, with little food and water, enduring intense heat, starvation, and shark attacks. A Japanese bomber's machine gunners once strafed the airmen, causing one raft to deflate and the other to be nearly destroyed.

After 33 days at sea, McNamara died, and Zamperini and the other castaways survived on rainwater and the odd catch bird or fish. However, their weight quickly dropped below 100 pounds. The Japanese Navy seized Zamperini and Phillips near the Marshall Islands after they drifted for two more weeks. At that point, the guys had drifted an incredible two thousand miles.

Upon returning to the Japanese mainland from his six weeks of captivity on Kwajalein, Zamperini was subsequently subjected to three separate interrogation centres and prisoner of war camps.

In the two years that followed, he endured almost daily beatings from guards in addition to diseases, exposure, and malnutrition. Japanese corporal Mutsuhiro Watanabe, affectionately known as "the Bird" among the prisoners of war, relished the opportunity to torture the runner.

While incarcerated at the Omori and Naoetsu prison camps, Mutsuhiro repeatedly threatened Zamperini's life and brutally attacked him with clubs, belts, and fists.

While in prison, he threatened to shoot Zamperini if the American man let go of a large wooden board held over his head, and he also made Zamperini and other American inmates fight until they were nearly all unconscious. Zamperini would go on to add that he kept an eye out for Mutsuhiro "like I was searching for a lion loose in the jungle."

Although his status as an Olympian protected him from the Japanese, it also made him an easy target for extra punishment. The guards at the Ofuna detention centre subjected a malnourished and frail Zamperini to foot races against Japanese opponents, and when he mustered the courage to win, they brutally beat him with clubs.

Radio Tokyo officials in Japan later tried to get him to read propaganda messages on the air by dragging him into their studio. The Japanese intended to exploit Zamperini—who had been left for dead back home—to bring down American morale and cast the United States administration in a negative light.

Zamperini was warned that he would be condemned to a punishment camp if he continued to cooperate, but he nevertheless agreed to recite a message informing his parents that he was alive.

Zamperini's Saving Journey

Even though he and his fellow prisoners of war were freed when the Japanese surrendered in September 1945, Zamperini's memories of the war would never fully leave him. After years of torment and starvation, he was unable to return to running and developed an alcohol dependency to cope with nightmares and memories.

In retrospect, Zamperini attributes his recovery from PTSD to hearing the gospel preacher Billy Graham in 1949. He then established a wilderness centre for disturbed adolescents and went on speaking tours across the country to share the story of his conversion to Christianity.

Zamperini made his first visit to Japan since his release in 1950 to speak to Japanese war criminals housed at Tokyo's Sugamo Prison.

There, he reunited with some of his former camp guards, shaking hands and embracing them. Zamperini attempted to meet with his former tormentor when in Nagano, Japan, for the 1998 Winter Olympics, but was unsuccessful. Zamperini wrote a letter later forgiving Mutsuhiro Watanabe, who had evaded capture.

In conclusion, Louis Zamperini's life was unique and difficult to classify. His astounding path from defiant child to Olympic athlete, prisoner of war to motivational speaker showcases the indomitable human spirit. With unflinching determination, he faced down hardship and came out on top every time.

It was impossible to ignore Zamperini's athletic accomplishments. After overcoming his personal struggles, he became a nationally acclaimed runner and competed in the 1936 Berlin Olympics.

Although he did not receive a medal, he made a lasting impression on the global platform. His status as a sporting icon was further cemented by the honours he got in his latter years, such as the renowned Louis Zamperini Invitational Mile and his induction into the National Italian American Sports Hall of Fame.

Zamperini's Forgiveness Legacy

The honours are important, but they are not the extent of Zamperini's legacy. Horrifying things happened to him throughout his service in the military. He demonstrated an incredible determination to live while stranded at sea, threatened with starvation and peril at every turn.

Despite going through unfathomable pain at the hands of his captors, he managed to muster the will to forgive. One of the strongest indicators that the human spirit may triumph over adversity is its capacity for forgiveness.

Zamperini spent his last years as an inspiration to everyone around him. In the process of becoming an inspiring motivational speaker, he reached an international audience with his tale of perseverance and forgiveness. Those at-risk youngsters, who were dealing with issues similar to his own turbulent past, appeared to be his primary concern.

The global success of the book and film "Unbroken" attests to the story's lasting impact; it has inspired and motivates innumerable people to face and conquer their own personal challenges.

Military service and athletic achievement were not the only facets of Louis Zamperini's life. He became an icon of perseverance, forgiveness, and inspiration, illuminating the limitless potential of the human spirit.

Details of his direct charitable activity may have faded with the passage of time, but his life after WWII reveals a profound commitment to serving others, especially at-risk youngsters.

Even though he was tragically thought to have died during the war, Louis Zamperini had a long and influential life despite this misfortune. Despite being 97 years old, he died quietly in 2014 at his Los Angeles home.

Conclusion

As we conclude the remarkable life story of Louis Silvie Zamperini, we are left with a profound sense of awe and admiration for a man who epitomized resilience, courage, and forgiveness in the face of unimaginable adversity.

Born in 1917 to Italian immigrants, Zamperini's journey from a talented high school athlete to an Olympic contender was just the beginning of a life that would be defined by extraordinary feats of endurance and determination. His record-breaking performances on the track captured the hearts of many, but it was his indomitable spirit that would truly leave a lasting impression on the world.

With the outbreak of World War II, Zamperini's life took a dramatic turn as he served as a bombardier in the Army Air Corps. His harrowing experience of being stranded at sea for 47 days after a plane crash, followed by years of brutal treatment as a prisoner of war in Japanese camps, tested his physical and mental strength to the utmost limit.

Yet, it was Zamperini's capacity for forgiveness that truly set him apart. Despite enduring unimaginable cruelty at the hands of his captors, he found it within himself to forgive them, a testament to his extraordinary character and resilience.

After the war, Zamperini's journey towards healing and redemption was marked by struggles with trauma and alcoholism. However, a pivotal moment at a Billy Graham sermon set him on a path towards recovery and renewal. He dedicated himself to helping others, establishing the Victory Boys Camp and extending forgiveness to his former captors.

Zamperini's story has inspired generations, captured in books and immortalized on the silver screen. His legacy as a survivor, a hero, and a symbol of forgiveness and redemption continues to resonate with people around the world.

As we bid farewell to Louis Zamperini, who passed away in 2014 at the age of 97, we are reminded that his spirit lives on in the hearts of those he touched. His story serves as a beacon of hope, reminding us that even in our darkest moments, there is always the possibility of redemption and forgiveness. Louis Zamperini may have left this world, but his legacy will endure for generations to come, a testament to the power of the human spirit to overcome the greatest of challenges.

Printed in Dunstable, United Kingdom